FOREVER SPICE

BY THE SPICE GIRLS PHOTOGRAPHY BY DEAN FREEMAN

Little, Brown & Company
Boston • New York • London

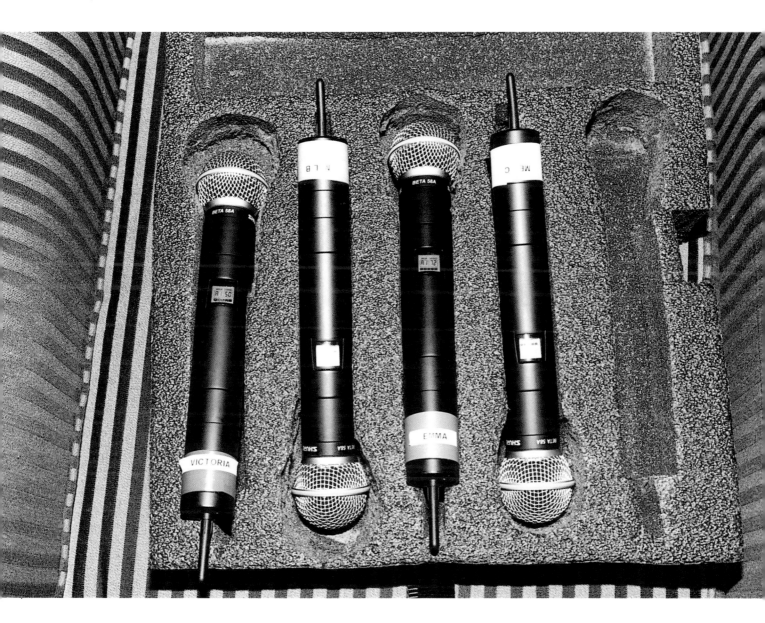

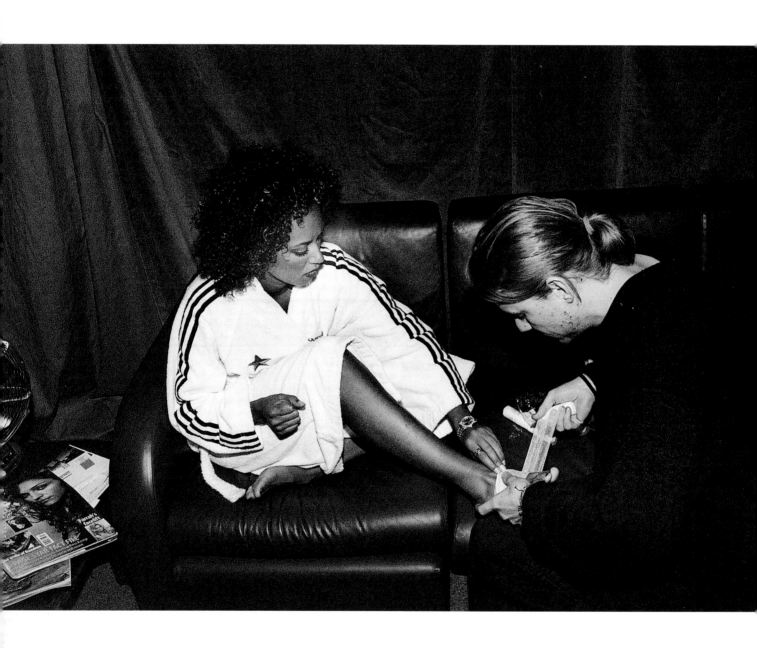

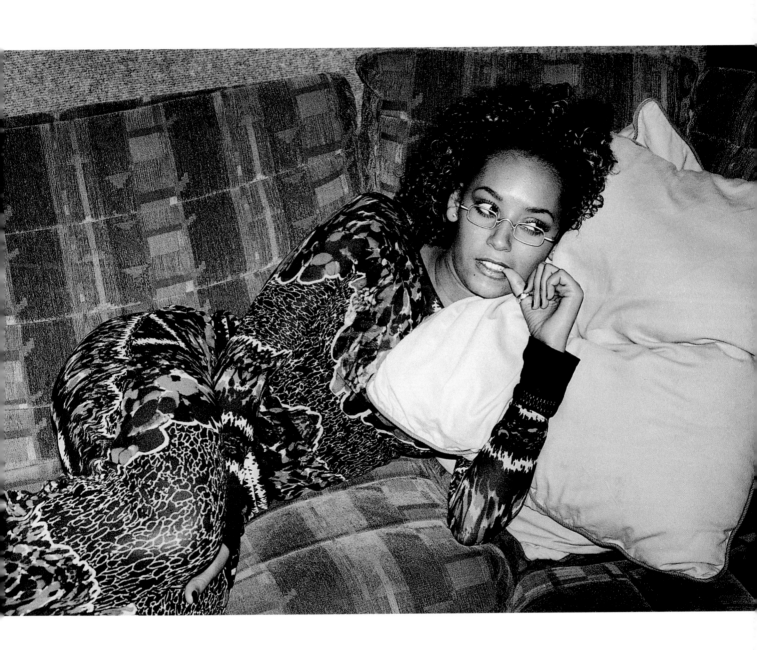

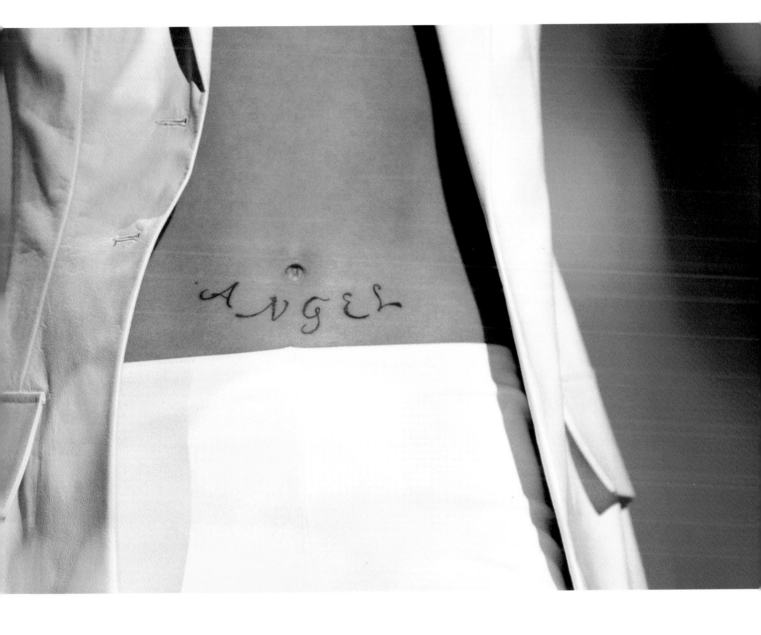

ON TOUR

Victoria

I was saying to one of the other Girls the other day that I can remember when we were standing in line at the dole office to collect our cheques and then the next time we were standing in that same line was when we were collecting our Brit awards. When I look back over the things that we've achieved, I'm still taken aback, totally.

Melanie C

'Goodbye' was originally about a relationship ending, but now it's about Geri and it's really sad.

Victoria (On tour 1998)

I really miss Geri a lot. Right at the beginning, I was really upset and gutted. The next minute I wanted to punch her in the head. It kept changing, from day to day. We'll get through it. I got on really well with Geri and I really like her. I will always be her friend.

Emma

One day we all sat down and talked about how we'd been working for such a long time. We came to a point where we said, "Okay, we definitely want to do another Spice album, but when the tour finishes in September, you never know, we might want to do our own thing for a while". Geri was the first to come to the group and say that she wanted to do her own thing. I remember being absolutely gutted and crying. We said, "That's cool, we all want to do that, so it's fine." But I remember feeling upset because I was worried that it might come to the point when she left. The rest of us were quite definite about doing another Spice album, whereas she wasn't.

It's strange, because the night before she left the band, we were laughing and joking around on a flight. Mel B was being a bit loud in the back and Geri and I were laughing about everything. And then the next day she was gone. I felt so angry. I wouldn't even expect my friend in Finchley to do that to me, and that's someone I haven't constantly been with for 5 years. First I was angry, then I was sad. I often really miss her.

It was quite hard. We'd done a lot of shows in Europe, but we were really quite nervous about America, so it was a bit of a kick in the teeth really. Even though she wasn't there, we still had interviews to do. Obviously we didn't know what to say, because we didn't know what was going on, so it was a difficult time.

Melanie C rang her and asked, "What's happened?" She said, "I can't come back." Mel and Victoria spoke to her again, saying, "But this is silly...". She still refused to come back. So we said, "Right, okay, we've got to go on." It was hard.

We'd planned everything in the show for five and had to re-arrange it for four. It wasn't that difficult. Professionally, okay, she wanted to go and we dealt with it. But we still haven't dealt with the friendship side. At home I've got this gorgeous big silver frame with a picture of Geri and me from Elle magazine. I haven't taken it down, like you do with pictures of old boyfriends. It won't ever come down because Geri was part of me and she always will be.

Melanie G (On tour 1998)

Geri leaving happened so quickly that we didn't really have time to think. We just had to get on with it, do the show, have the party. It just happened really fast. It didn't really sink in until after the two shows in Oslo, when we had something like ten days off. Emma and I went on holiday with our mums and my sister and had a really relaxing time. Then it was like, "Whoah! Hold on a minute!" For a while there was always someone missing, but then obviously you kick start back into the professionalism and get on with it.

You'd lost someone, so that felt a bit bad. Well, really bad, actually. I had times when I felt lonely without her, because she was my mate. There are times when you go over and over it in your head, but then a part of you says, stop torturing yourself, get on with it, you've got a job to do. Otherwise you'd just be down and depressed and asking questions that can't be answered, because she's not here to answer them.

Melanie C (On tour 1998)

Thankfully we've been very busy, so we didn't have a lot of time to think about it when Geri first left. But it really hit home when we had a few days off. We were just gutted, we couldn't even get out of bed. You know, when you feel just so deflated, absolutely deflated. It was like you had just lost a part of you, like a death. And on stage it was hard because there is always interaction in the show and there was quite a lot between Geri and me. For the first few shows it was really weird because I kept thinking, where is she?

I have grieved and I don't feel any animosity towards her at all. I now respect her decision and hope that whatever she does in the future works out well for her. I went through a phase when I couldn't look at her picture without feeling anxious, but now if I see her I just think, it's our Geri.

Melanie G
The first few times on stage without Geri were strange. Obviously we had to share out the lines she sang between us and sometimes I'd forget to sing her lines.

Victoria

In a way, I think that Geri leaving gave us all a kick up the bum. It made you think, right, you can't relax too much. You've really got to work hard because you've got a point to prove. But no matter what anybody says, it was still one of our friends who'd abandoned us and I felt very lonely after she'd gone.

Victoria

I always got on very well with Geri and I wish her luck in what she's doing now, but I was totally shocked when she left the band. My sister had just had Liberty and I was on my way to see them at the hospital when we got the call from the lawyer.

Luckily America went exceptionally well. It could really have been a bad time for us and there were a lot of people trying to be negative, but on the other hand I was quite surprised at how positive people in the media were. I thought that everyone would say it was the end of the Spice Girls again, so I was quite surprised when they didn't. And now I feel a bit sorry for Geri.

Victoria

I feel much more in control since we sacked our manager. We're much happier doing it the way we're doing it now. We've got a lovely office and really nice people working with us. Now we make our own decisions because that's the way we've always wanted it.

Emma

Looking back now, I'm not sure what Simon really wanted to do. I don't know whether he wanted to make as much money out of us as he could, because he didn't think we were going to last ... or what. Leaving him when we did was definitely best for the group. Anyway, I tend never to regret anything. I think things always happen for a reason. We'd got to the point where we knew we could do it on our own.

When we originally went to him, we went as us, the Girls. All the ideas came from us and we already had a lot of tracks. We wanted a manager to elevate us to that next level and help us become international, not someone who was going to take over completely. That wasn't what we were about, but we all sort of humoured him, in a way. Deep down, we knew what he was doing. It was obvious that he wanted this group to be perfect, in its own little bubble, without any outside influences. And we wanted to be big and put our music across. Writing our own stuff was really important to us and if he was helping us get there, then so be it.

Melanie G

If I saw Simon in the street I'd definitely say hello to him, I don't feel bitter towards him at all because he did a lot of good, whatever else he did. Mentally it might have gone a bit wrong for all of us with him, but as far as managers go, he was fantastic. He got us out there and made us internationally known. He knew exactly what he was doing.

Leaving him was one of those things that was just going to happen. If it hadn't happened then, it would have happened within the next couple of months. It was just time to move on. When people start having different visions, you either have to correct them or go your own way.

I just think he didn't get where we were at. We were slowly being separated and we needed to get back to each other. We'd had success very, very quickly and it was time to sit down and begin to understand yourself and each other, not have someone demanding more work from you. You have to give breathing space and growing time to adjust to what's happened. It was a strange time.

It was heading that way for a while, but we decided to leave him the night before we did MTV. Something was gonna happen, whether it be a big argument or a bust up - it was bubbling under.

Simon would make you very aware that it was dangerous to go out. He was trying to create that superstar thing, which is one thing that we said we'd never be. We want to be accessible, we want to be reachable, we want to go and do our supermarket shopping, we want to fend for ourselves. He was cocooning us in cotton-wool, which is alright for a while, but then you just feel like an alien.

His philosophy was that you can't let boyfriends come out and see you much because it distracts you from your work. He had a point, but if your work is important to you, nothing distracts you. He didn't believe that we were strong and confident enough for it to be like that.

Melanie C

I think we'd all been feeling that we'd like to leave Simon for a long, long time, but we were too frightened to admit it to each other. When someone actually brought the subject up and we eventually took the plunge, we were all in full agreement that it had to be done.

The others were more shocked at my reaction than anybody else's. Melanie and Geri were really worried because they were the first to go to each other and say, "Something's got to be done!" They thought that I might be apprehensive about leaving him because I like security. But I was as unhappy as the rest of them. They said, "We think we should leave Simon," and I said, "So do I!" They were amazed.

Melanie C (On tour 1998)

The day we left Simon was such a huge release for me. Until that day I'd feel guilty if I didn't go to the gym every day, but now if I don't feel like going (which is pretty rare), I don't go and I don't care.

I still go to the gym and I do get angry with myself at times because I am not as dedicated as I used to be. But I went too far back then. I think that was because it was the only control I had. I went completely teetotal and would never, ever eat anything naughty. Now I am in control of my whole life, I've loosened up a bit and even have a drink now and then. Now it's like, so what?

Emma

Before the tour, we rehearsed for three weeks in Ireland. It was really hard work, especially for Mel G and me because we hated the gym, but we had to get fit for the tour. Singing and dancing is fine, because you're expressing yourself, but the gym is so boring. We had a trainer and he gave Mel and me special classes because he knew we were lazy. Melanie C, Geri and Victoria would go in the morning but Mel and I hate mornings, so we'd have to do it either before our dance class or after. Sometimes we didn't go and then we'd feel really guilty. But even without the gym, the days were very long and I'd end up in bed at 10pm, just absolutely shattered. Then the boys joined us and that was quite a laugh. I remember us coming back from rehearsals and saying, "The boys are here! Let's go and see what they look like!"

Melanie C

We were all dancers before we became Spice Girls, so it was nice to have the dancers around. We're all the same breed. We know all the same people and seem to have the same mentality, or we're all mental!

Emma

We always say that nobody knew the high we got on stage. That feeling of coming off and looking at each other and thinking, we've just done the show and it was great and we got a great response from the audience! Obviously there are lovely people coming in and saying, "It was brilliant" and "That was lovely", but they don't know. Sometimes we just screamed our heads off because we'd just done a show and we knew what each one of us was feeling. It was fabulous. This was just after the first show: "Yeah, we did it. We're on our way!" We were so excited.

Melanie G

This was in Ireland and we all had these silky dressing gowns that Kenny found for us. They were baby blue and silky - eeugh! - but we wore them religiously, even Victoria.

Melanie C

It was after the first show and we were just so excited because we'd done it. There was a camera crew there and a film crew, so we were showing off and being really hyper. We just kept singing, "We are family!" from the last song of the show.

Emma

We were really nervous on the first night, especially because all our families were there. I always say that you can perform to thousands of people without a second thought, but when there's just one person in the audience you know, it's much more nerve-racking. The first night was the hardest, but we were always nervous before a show, especially Melanie C. You just think of silly things like, I hope I don't fall over today, or, I've got to hit that note tonight. Still, I just tried to make it fun and enjoy myself. If you get too nervous, it overtakes you a bit and works against you.

Melanie G (On Tour 1998)

I like travelling, but not on really long trips. I think it would be nice to travel when you want, to say, "Oh, I'm bored today, so I'm just going to pop off to America and do a show." It would be great just to do one show a week and have the rest of the time off. We don't have any time to ourselves on tour - we do a show, then rush on to the next city to do another show, with the occasional day off. But even when we have a day off, we're thinking about the show for the next day. I'd like time off just to do nothing and think about nothing! It's important to have enough time to decide what you want and what you need to be happy.

I don't actually feel 'home-sick' because I haven't lived at home for ages and I've just bought a new house. Mostly I miss everyday things, like meeting a friend to go for a drink in Leeds or London. I miss the life I have there, even just driving in my car on my way to see Rebecca or driving home. But I try to keep myself in a good mood all the time by calling home and doing interesting things on my days off.

Melanie C (On tour 1998)

Touring is wicked but the travelling is a nightmare - staying in different hotels and getting up at 5.00 a.m. to catch a bus or a plane. You get so tired, and when you are down the vibe can be quite low for the day. Then we might have a really good show and go straight back up on a high again. It's just up and down, up and down.

After all this time on the road, it's impossible not to feel homesick. I miss my family and friends, I miss my gym, I miss going to the supermarket and having a routine. Food suddenly becomes majorly important. On tour you have catering and so you can have anything you want, really, but you just miss little things like home cooking, Flora or Hovis bread - just silly things like that. I miss TV like Eastenders and Coronation Street, too. And I have no idea what's happening on the music scene back home. I think you have to be in a country to feel the vibe of that country at the time.

Victoria (On tour 1998)

I try not to watch sad films when I'm away because I get really homesick. Emma and I get the most homesick out of everybody. I cry every day because I want to go home. I hate being away from home.

I get home and I think, god, I've missed all of this. My brother's suddenly really tall and he's got a beard. My sister has just given birth and is now a mother. I've missed seeing them grow up and I can't help thinking, where has that chunk of life gone? Oh yeah, I was away travelling the world, which is great and fantastic and everything, but I'm so close to my family that all I ever do when I am not working is phone my mum.

I am so close to my mum and sister. I called home the other day and my mum said, "Your sister has just come in with the baby!" I could hear baby noises and then they put up this swing in the lounge for the baby. It swings the baby to sleep and plays musical tunes and I could hear all this in the background. I could hear EastEnders on the TV in the background and then my dad came in from the chip shop with everybody's dinner. My brother had just got back from work and I could hear the other phone ringing and it was my sister's friend. I was here on my own. Okay, we're famous and we're doing what we enjoy, but all I was thinking at the time was, god I miss my family and home! I miss seeing the windows all steamy when my mum has burnt the dinner and there's a chair wedging the door open so that the fire alarm doesn't go off.

I have been strong for a long time and you always think to yourself, come on, let's be strong, let's move on. But I don't want to be strong any more. I just want to sit down and cry and for someone to say, "You don't have to worry any more. I will be strong for you." I'm fed up with being in a battle all the time and having to put my shield up in front of me each day. I just want to lie down and have someone stand in front of me with their shield and say, "I'll protect you."

Emma

I didn't get too homesick because we were very busy most of the time. But when I wasn't busy, I really missed home. I missed silly things like watching Blind Date and getting ready to go out with the girls. I remember doing that when I got back and I thought it was so exciting.

The homesickness obviously gets easier near the end of a tour because you're thinking, okay I've only got this much longer. Europe was easier because you could go home between gigs, but harder because of that, too. You were going home and coming back and going again. When we left for America, with three months touring ahead of us, we had a cry. Then Victoria and I said, "But this is the last time we have to say goodbye to anybody." Whereas before it was always, "Okay, bye again, I'm going again" and then "I'm back, okay I'm going again." But this time it was like, "Next time I see you I'm home for good", so it was okay. We always try to put a positive slant on things.

Melanie G

That day was absolutely mental. We had all these security men walking alongside us, but they were asking for our autographs in the middle of it all. They were supposed to be there protecting us from fans, but just because they were in uniform, they managed to get closer than the fans did.

Emma

It's actually quite nice to have minders with you because it gives you a real sense of security. I found that if I was walking along the street on my own, people would be saying, "Is it..?" But if I was with Mel, they'd definitely know it was us, so we had to have people around. I drive myself around in England on my own, but America is a lot more intense, so it was good to have someone to keep an eye on us.

Melanie C

Our minders are really cool because they're very discreet. But sometimes if you're using security in Europe or America, they get a bit heavy-handed and hustle and bustle and push everybody out of the way, which is really embarrassing. You feel a bit of an idiot when that happens.

Victoria

We all looked after each other on tour and we sort of shared mums as well. So when someone's mum came to see us, she would be like a mum to the rest of us, too.

Melanie C

I didn't really party a lot on tour. The girls know how disciplined I am and I've always been that way. We just really accept and respect each other the way that we are. But the funny thing is, when I do go out and party, I'm out later than everybody else. I was always the one dancing on the tables at the end of the night when everyone else was in bed. I can party harder than all of them put together! It's just that I like doing it in the right time and place.

Emma

I remember the tour as loads and loads of fun and partying and being around lots of people. Obviously if I look back properly, there were times when I was very tired, but I mainly remember the good times. It was just brilliant and I loved it.

Maybe I got through it more easily than the other Girls because I'm younger than them! (Not really!) I often hook up with two of the dancers, Louie and Carmine, and we reminisce all the time, even about the nights when we'd stay in and get room service and all watch a film. There'd be six of us lying on the bed watching a video - it was just great fun.

Louie and Carmine are now two of my best friends and we're always together, which is cool. They're the ones I've stayed in contact with, even though I made friends with all the crew and band. When we went out, after shows, there would literally be the whole band, all the dancers and the crew and it would just be madness.

We reminisce about the times when Mel B and I went on the tour bus, which was always a laugh. There was one night after a show when we were so hungry that we headed straight for MacDonalds. We were a bit late and they'd just closed and we were banging on the door shouting, "Pleeeeease open up. We're Spice Girls! We'll give you autographs! We need Big Macs!" It was really hilarious.

Emma

Europe was easier for everybody because it wasn't so far away from home. If we had a weekend off, we could fly home. Also, a lot of Europe is very beautiful and cultural and the food's great. America was much harder work than Europe, so we spent more time sitting in rooms, watching telly and getting room service than going out. But that was nice, too.

We tried to do as much as we could in America. It's a place I'd always wanted to go to and I did enjoy it, but we zipped through so quickly that it was hard to take a lot of it in. The best day for me was when a load of us went to Disney World in Florida. The whole band, all the dancers and a lot of the crew came and we had a brilliant day. We didn't have to queue for anything and we had food every five minutes, so it was just brilliant!

We went on the Space Mountain about three times and then we felt sick. The others went on this big ride called Aliens, where you walk along next to huge aliens. I've got a phobia about big things (like aeroplanes), so I was like, "I'm not going on this!" so I sat outside on my own for about 15 minutes feeling like a real idiot instead. I loved funfairs as a kid. I was always on the big rides like the big wheel and my mum used to hate it, so she'd have to find someone else for me to go with.

One day there was a big outing to Niagara Falls, but I didn't go in the end. I ended up sunbathing with Victoria and Mel and going to the cinema to see Cinderella starring Drew Barrymore. I just wanted to do a bit of chilling that day.

Melanie C

We had a wonderful plane. It was quite big because we had so many people travelling with us. We had a nice host and hostess to look after us and prepare all our favourite foods. We were always starving after the gig. I used to have loads of sushi and fruit and they'd do special stuff like tortilla wraps and chicken wings and always lots of cereal.

You get used to flying. Once you're hardened to travelling, it sort of sticks, even if you don't go anywhere for a while. It's quite nice sometimes, because it's the only time you can relax. There's not much you can do on an aeroplane.

Melanie G

When I look back, I just see the tour as complete madness. We were constantly on the go, in different towns, different hotels, rushing around in cars and planes and meeting all kinds of different people. It was manic. But even though it was manic, it felt quite normal and safe because we were always with the same people, who became our extended family in a way. Everyone was on the same happy vibe because it was sunny a lot of the time and that always brings out the best in people, I think. Good times.

It was exciting because we were always on the move and never got too familiar with one place. We also had some great days out, to Disney World and Niagara Falls, with all the crew. In Europe we'd go out every night in a big gang and often we'd just take over the place. It was brilliant. One night five of us went and had tattoos done by our mate Claudio, who worked right through the night to do them all. That was when I had the extra signs done on my stomach.

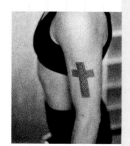

Melanie C

I had a couple of tattoos done while I was on the tour. I had my ANGEL put on my belly in Milan and had another one done on the base of my spine in America. I'd always wanted tattoos because I think they look really cool. The one round my arm is a Celtic band and it was the first one I had done. It shows allegiance to your tribe, so I think of mine as showing my allegiance to the Spice Girls. Once you've had one tattoo, you get addicted and immediately start thinking about the next one you're going to have. So then I had some Japanese characters put above my Celtic band, because I like the way they look. The symbols mean 'Woman' and 'Strength' - Girl Power! It's funny, though, because I met a Japanese girl who told me that the 'Woman' symbol is on every female toilet in Japan!

I felt a bit lopsided with two tattoos on my right arm, so I had one done on my left arm next. I've always liked crosses and a Celtic cross is lucky and protects you, so that's what I chose. Then I'd always wanted a written tattoo, but I didn't know where to put it. In the end I thought my belly would be a good place, because it would give me the incentive to keep it in shape.

Melanie C

I lost my grandfather and step-grandma to cancer while I was on tour. I always feel like they're my guardian angels looking after me, so I wanted something to signify that I still think about them, even though they're not here anymore. So that's why my belly tattoo says ANGEL. For the last one, on the base of my spine, I wanted something that was quite earthy. Anthony from Red Hot Chili Peppers helped me design it, using the Tibetan symbol for 'Grounding'. Often I like the look of something and only later find out that it's actually very meaningful. And as time goes by, these tattoos have more and more meaning for me.

It was very hard when my grandparents died because I couldn't be with my family. Then again, it was good to be busy because it meant I didn't dwell on it too much. Sometimes it was quite magical actually, because even though I'd be on stage with a whole host of other people, I was still able to feel a kind of solitude up there. You can be

Emma

We saw each other most days, but we gave each other space, too. There were odd days obviously when David was over and you'd think, right, leave them. They've only got two days.

Melanie C

It was nice when the other girls had their boyfriends out because I like them to be happy - and it gets them off my back! It also gives me a chance to be on my own, which I like. I get on well with all the lads, too.

Victoria

I'd quite often socialise with the other Girls on a day off, even if it was just to sit in each other's rooms and order room service or go for a walk or go shopping.

We went out for dinner quite a lot, too. Melanie and Emma were the ones who went out clubbing, whereas, if anything, I'd probably sit in with Mel C and watch a video.

The great thing is that I can totally be myself with them, all the time. We know each other so well, and we've all seen each other happy, sad, crying, whatever, that we're totally comfortable with one another. It takes a while to get to that stage in a friendship, but living together gives you a good foundation. We lived together in a house in Maidenhead for nearly a year, so we were close friends before we became famous. That was good because we all knew what it was like to really long for it, so then it's great when it happens and you've got other people to enjoy it with. Also, you understand the highs and lows of it all, so that brings you closer together.

Melanie C

I could never be uncomfortable around the other Girls. Even if there's a silence, it's never an embarrassing silence. We can do absolutely anything in front of each other, even poo. We've been together for ages so we're more like sisters than friends. We're always cuddling and hugging each other. And it's okay to push each other away, too, if you're not in the mood. You can say, "Oh, get off!" and no one's offended because we know we love each other really.

Melanie C

Everyone shouted at me for wearing a Brazil top, but we were out of the World Cup anyway, so I don't know what the fuss was about.

An empty auditorium still has a real vibe because of all the past concerts and blood, sweat and tears it's witnessed. There's always a little magic there, but you just can't compare it to when it's full of people. The venues don't actually look that big when they're empty, but when they're full of people and the faraway ones are like little dots, you realise just how huge they are.

Melanie G

We didn't have much of a routine. The only bit that was always the same was before the gig: you do a sound check then you eat, get ready, do your sit-ups, get your hair and make-up done and go on stage. Apart from that, every day was different.

Melanie C

We wrote almost every song we performed on tour, so every single word matters when you're singing it. It's our story, it's my story, they're my words, they're our words. When I sing 2 Become 1 I'm thinking about someone and feeling real emotions about something that's happened. It's not a vibe you get into, it just happens naturally. It would be harder not to do it.

Emma

This was Wembley, the day we did the shoot for the football song. I was probably thinking, what have I got on my feet?

Melanie C

I don't know how any of them danced in those silly shoes.

up there in that top corner, singing a little verse in front of tens of thousands of people, but you can still feel alone. It's at times like that when you can sense a special presence. My grandad loved 'Viva Forever' and sometimes when we sang it on stage, I felt like he was there and I was singing it just to him.

My grandparents were both ill with cancer for a long time, so we knew we were going to lose them, but it was still really sad. We were in France in March when I got the phone call. My mum had to go straight home and then shortly after she got home, my grandad passed away. It was awful to be away from home, but luckily the Girls were there. They were great and really looked after me.

Victoria

David's probably saying, "Are you sure you want to wear that wig tonight? You do realise it's awful, don't you?" The girls bought me that bracelet for my birthday. It's Tiffanys and it's got diamonds in it.

Emma

The fans varied a lot, depending on where we were. Europe was a lot of boys, often older boys and quite screamy and good fun, actually. On the other hand, the English audiences were quite young. The Americans scream and sing along, but in Europe they're a bit feistier and the sound coming from them was far deeper.

Victoria

I prefer the audiences in Europe. They're really mad, with lots of wild screaming at the front. I found the audiences more reserved in America. Also, we played a lot of venues in the middle of nowhere, in places I hadn't heard of. It took a lot longer to get to the venues in America, too. We'd have to fly for ages, then get on a bus and drive for ages because we had such huge distances to cover. I preferred the food in Europe, especially since you can usually find a Marks & Spencer there, and it does make a big, big difference when there's a huge time gap and you want to pick up the phone and ring somebody. You can't just ring - you have to work out the difference and often wait for hours before they're up. As much as it was good fun, to me America was very, very difficult.

Melanie G

Sometimes it was the mothers dressing up as us, and sometimes the kids. Sometimes the front row would be filled with older people and you'd see them sitting down at the start of the show, then after a couple of songs they'd be really going for it! Everyone, grandads, kids, mums... everyone. It was brilliant to see, absolutely brilliant. Every show, we'd point somebody out, "Oi, you!" and get the cameraman to put them on the big screen. "You're not dancing! You're not smiling! Come on, stand up!" And they'd have to stand up in front of everyone. It was quite funny.

One of the best audiences we had was on the night of my dad's birthday. I had a party for him because it's his birthday on the 28th May and mine on the 29th. It was just after Geri left, so it was good that there was something other than just that going on. I had my dad's ears pierced and I had everybody in the room watching him as it happened.

Melanie C

Our fans are just absolutely mad everywhere. Absolutely mad. They were so receptive at every gig. Manchester and New York were probably the toughest audiences, but they were still an absolute dream and we brought the house down.

We had the party round at my suite and the theme was cowboy style. You all had to wear jeans and a white t-shirt and, when you walked in, you were either given a cowboy hat or a bandanna or a sheriff's badge to wear. So that was really fun.

Emma

I remember this. We were in South Africa and we took over the whole place and started playing all the bongos. And I think we ate crocodile there as well. It tasted like chicken.

Melanie G

Lots of funny things would happen on stage, like when Melanie C split her trousers right at the start of the show and had to stay on for the next three numbers.

Victoria

One night a great big sticky moth flew into my hair and got stuck there. I didn't know what to do. I had to run offstage and get someone to yank it out.

Another embarrassing thing that happened to me on tour was in a hotel room somewhere. I'd got a fizzy water out of the mini-bar and I couldn't find a bottle opener anywhere. It wasn't in the mini-bar, or the bathroom and there I was thinking: "Where on earth would you put the opener?" Finally, I found it attached to the wall, hanging from a big old rusty chain. I gave it a pull - and the whole wall fell down. It was terrible - it stank like nothing else.

Melanie G

We always made sure we made the most of our days off and did things like have a picnic at Niagara Falls, wearing stupid cagoules. If Emma woke up depressed, or I woke up depressed, the other one would say, "Come on, let's do something!" Everyone enjoyed going on those days out because we got VIP treatment, which was brilliant. It was great to be able to take everyone round Disney World and not queue. You wouldn't want to do it by yourself because you'd feel stupid, but with a group of 20 it was excellent.

I remember all the shows like they were yesterday. Something bizarre always happened. One night a pigeon flew onto the stage and I couldn't get rid of it. It followed me around for the entire gig and really started to freak me out. In Arizona, we played a couple of gigs in the middle of the desert. At the end of 'Sisters', Mel and I usually fall on the floor and one night in Arizona we opened our eyes and saw loads of crickets on stage! It was horrific. Another night there were masses of weird flying things zooming around in the air. You'd be singing away and suddenly a huge buzzing insect would hit you in the face. It was mad.

Other times, one of us would drop the mic or start crying in the middle of a song or suddenly see the same person again, for the 10th night in a row. We'd subtly let each other know what was going on, which was often quite funny. And then we'd do wind-ups on each other. When it was my turn to introduce a song, I'd sometimes say: "And Victoria has something really important to tell you!" She'd hiss: "What?" and have to make something up on the spot. We'd always try to get each other back for tricks like that. The other Girls got me back big time in Sheffield for all the times that I'd put them in sticky situations. It was 12th September, the day before I got married, and they made Jim come on stage and propose to me in front of everybody. Usually when they put

me in a sticky situation, I'd blag my way right out, but I couldn't do much about it that time.

We always had a lot of fun just before 'Sisters'. Emma and Victoria would come on stage and say: "We've lost the two Mels - does anybody know where they are?" while Mel and I were quickly getting changed into our rock outfits. Then they'd go off stage and Mel and I would have a proper banter backstage. The audience could hear us, but they didn't have a clue where we were. We said something different every night. Melanie would pretend that she was up in the balcony and say: "Get off me you wazzak! No, I won't sign your autograph! Go home!" And the audience wouldn't know where her voice was coming from. It was a real laugh.

There was loads of action backstage where we got changed. We had our own cubicles, but the dancers didn't, so Louis and Carmine would take Polaroids of themselves and stick them up in our dressing rooms. Melanie had her whole cubicle dedicated to Liverpool F. C. and Vicky had David splattered all over hers. There always used to be a funny smell in mine and I could never work out why until, at the end of the tour, Carmine told me that my dresser had a farting problem. For ages, I thought it was me, so I was quite relieved.

There were all kinds of things going on with the dressers. Sometimes they'd get on with each other, sometimes they wouldn't. There was quite a lot of tension between them as to who was the quickest dresser. If one of them got, say, Mel C dressed first, whoever was the slowest would be in a bad mood for the rest of that half of the show. It was really funny, really funny.

If one of the band had, had a really hard core night out on the town the night before, we'd pick on him throughout the show. One of them was seeing one of the caterers and sometimes we'd slip that in when we introduced the band. "And now we've got Fergus on the drums and he's seeing Michelle from catering!" But you'd say it so quickly that only they'd know what you'd said. Nobody else would pick up on it.

Melanie C

My ponytail went flying off one night at Wembley, the most important gig, of course. It was funny. That's what I love about live shows - it's there and it's then and if it goes wrong it's over and done with and you move on. But when you're being filmed and it's there forever, it's a bit scary.

When you're a dancer and part of a corps it's like, the show must go on, no matter what. Nobody can know that something's gone wrong. But the nice thing about being a personality is that you can share your mistakes with the audience - you can laugh at yourself and make them laugh with you, which is nice.

We often used to ask each other: "Shall we do an encore tonight?". Sometimes you're just knackered and you think, God, we've got to go on and do another four numbers! But we did it every time. Every time. And when one of us was like: "Oh I really can't be bothered with this show", another would say: "Come on, we've only got (however many) shows left and it's gonna be over soon." We always egg each other on like that.

Sometimes I felt a bit down when I realised I had 90 more shows to do, even though it's brilliant and the buzz up there is fantastic. It was just that, once you've had a good show, you think, I've got to do that 90 times again and I can't not give it my all because all these people are paying money to see us. Once you get up on stage, you do it anyway, but sometimes you felt like you were in prison ticking off the days.

But I wasn't homesick. I didn't have a boyfriend at home. I didn't even have a house at home because I'd packed in my flat. I was living out of a suitcase. I had nothing tying me to home apart from my family and they all came out to see me a couple of times. So I was in quite a good position compared with Vicky and Emma, who missed their mums and boyfriends. Mel C and I were far freer that way. I loved it, because I knew that once I got back, I was going find somewhere to settle down.

Emma

We always had a really good laugh on the tour bus and there was always a spare bed for Mel and me. The American bus was fantastic. You had tellies in your bunk and Louie would be on the other side and we'd be watching telly and eating sweets. Then it'd be, "Stop! We need to get out and get some pizza!"

Melanie G

Eighty percent of the time, Emma and I were on the dancer's bus, but the rest of the time, we flew on the private plane. It was a totally different environment, with Molly and her boyfriend doing the catering and delicious food, like a cheese selection or some sushi. A couple of times the whole band came on the plane, too, because otherwise they would have been travelling for something like 48 hours to get to the venue. Once it was two members of the band's birthdays, so we had a big hoo-ha on the plane. It was brilliant. It was a great place to relax and stuff your face after a gig. One of the best things about having your own plane is that you're the only people on it. And you don't have to go through all that boring safety routine.

The journey from the airport to the gig or hotel was always quite interesting - and sometimes it was really bizarre. You'd be in somewhere like Oklahoma, where the only radio station for miles around was a country station. All the way to the hotel you'd have to sit and listen to country, mainly because you want the music loud so the driver doesn't hear about what you were doing at a party last night or this, that or the other. We'd be sitting there, asking, "Umm...Is this the only radio station they've got here?" Then the driver would flick through the stations, but it would all be the same music. In some places there was no R&B, just really strange folk tunes. And you could guarantee that nine times out of ten, the driver would turn round and say, "Can I have your autograph?"

When you're on the bus, you're on the bus for ten hours and in that time you can eat, have a walk around, have a bit of sleep and watch TV. On a plane you're up in the air for 40 minutes, 50 minutes at the most. You've got all that dehydration, then you have to get off the plane, get to the hotel, find your luggage, sleep, get up and repack. So half the time it was easier just to stay on the bus. But I think the bunks were too small for Victoria ... and it was a bit smelly, even though Louie had his little Hoover.

When you're travelling on the plane, as soon as that last number finishes, you run out to the bus in your costume or you change quickly and then get on the bus to the plane. You're in rush, rush, rush mode. But when you go with the dancers, you take your time, you all chill out, get a sandwich, have a shower and watch the stage being ripped down into pieces.

Mostly, you have to enjoy being on tour, even though there were times when I absolutely hated it. I just wanted a bit of peace somewhere for a couple of days, but I couldn't go anywhere, because I had to be there for the next gig.

Sometimes we did a bit of promotion before we went on stage, which was often fantastic, but occasionally you'd be interviewed by a real sexist journalist who just didn't get it, and that would put you in a bad mood. You'd have to shake it off really quickly, though, because you'd have to go out there and perform almost immediately afterwards.

Emma

We have this ritual before we go on stage and we're very superstitious about making sure we do it, no matter what. We always stand in the same formation, put our fists over each other's fists and shout and gear each other up.

Melanie C

We continued to do our pre-show ritual when Geri left. All for one and one for all! We did it on the first night and went on to do it every single night of the tour. Towards the end, we started becoming a bit more laid back about getting up on stage and it'd be, "Okay girls, 2 minute call" and we'd reply, "Yeah, alright," although we weren't even dressed. Suddenly it would be, "Oh my god, the show's started!" but we'd still insist, "We've got to do it, we've still got to do it!" It was as though we felt that not doing it would be a bad omen.

Melanie C

This was my favourite part of the show, when the doors opened. You can sense when they're fully open because the light changes to a bright light through your eyelids. That's when you open your eyes.

I kept them shut until then to get the full impact of seeing ten thousand people at once. It's more of a rush that way and it gets all your adrenaline pumping before you start singing If U Can't Dance.

Melanie G

You can be standing there in a foul mood, but as soon as the doors open, everything changes. You get straight into it because it's your music playing and you feel you've got to give the audience everything. Even if you don't want to give your all, you end up doing it, because you're on a roller coaster of high energy.

Emma

Melanie C would be concentrating completely while Mel G and I kept pushing each other and messing around just before the doors opened. We both had heels on, so if either of us had lost our balance, we'd have fallen over. Still, we did it for a little giggle just before the audience saw us. Then, when you see the crowd, it's just like, oh my god! The dancers used to watch from a gap in the stairs backstage and Louie said that he'd see us pushing each other or having a laugh, but then, as the doors opened, the grin on my face went from ear to ear. It was incredible - that whole feeling is just amazing.

Before we came on there was a big intro on the screens we were standing behind. You could hear the audience getting louder and louder during the build-up and then when the doors opened they broke into an overwhelming roar. It was fabulous, every single night.

Just before the doors opened, Emma and I used to push each until the very last second before we could be seen by the audience. Sometimes, I had an arm out or we'd still be pushing each other and suddenly we'd have to straighten up into our positions. It was always really funny to see whether we could contain ourselves.

Emma

By America, we'd got to know the show really well and so we mucked around more, which gave it more character. We'd got to know the dancers and every night we'd do something different. Either the boys would shock us or we'd shock them. We always had a laugh and I think that when you're enjoying yourself on the stage, it really gives off a different vibe to the audience.

Emma

I don't know where Melanie C got her energy from. Sometimes I'd feel so tired, after a show the night before and a plane journey, and she'd still be leaping around, like a nutter. We'd say, "Mel, can you just calm down? You're making us look really awful!"

Melanie G

One night I sprained my ankle. It was at the end of the show, when the music goes really, really mad. At that point, Victoria and I had this habit of grabbing each other's hands and swinging each other round like the clappers. Well, she accidentally let go and I went swinging off and sprained my ankle. I was crying my eyes out going up the steps and then I had to be carried off stage. It was nothing major, but it really hurt. The next night I had to go on stage with it strapped up, big time. I could hardly move it, but I managed.

Melanie C

I really liked doing "Sisters" with Mel because it's really rocky and we could just jump around and be nutters. I've not got good elevation, but I was always trying to jump as high as Damon from Blur. Melanie got injured one night and had a bad ankle for a few shows after that. She was carried off stage and had quite a bad sprain, but she soldiered on to the end of the show.

Melanie G (On Tour 1998)

I love doing the duet with Mel C. We had the idea to do it about six months ago. It's brilliant and vibey and it really gets the adrenaline going. You can really go for it visually, too, because although it's vocally set, the dance isn't a set routine, so we just run about being nutters on the stage. It's good to have a partner in crime, too!

Emma

We were at Wembley stadium, just about to go on stage, and we were listening to the chart countdown. It was brilliant when we heard Melanie G and Missy were No.1 and we all had a boogie to the song. To see one of your best friends have a No.1 was just lovely.

Victoria

We're all really proud of each other. That's the nice thing, you know, you can be pleased for people and not jealous of them.

Melanie G

I really enjoyed doing I Want You Back. I needed to do a track like that because that's what I've always wanted to do. I wondered if I could do a track by myself and feel proud of it. The night it was announced on the radio at Wembley, it didn't quite register, because I was about to go on stage. I was in show mode and it was almost embarrassing, really. I tried to shut everyone up, but the Girls made a big thing of it. "Everybody come in for the countdown!" It was quite mad. Everyone was jumping up and down and dancing and screaming.

Emma

This was in Italy and I think we'd been out before the gig. We always made time for shopping! My wardrobe changed quite a lot while I was over there. We were very lucky and Versace would invite us into the shop to get some stuff and so I'd be chucking out old Top Shop stuff and hanging up the Versace. I shipped back a few bits and pieces from the tour, but I wasn't like Melanie G. She went mad!

Victoria

I don't spend half as much time shopping as people think I do. I go to a shop, see an outfit and buy it, but I don't go out for long shopping days. I like nice clothes but I'd much prefer to have them delivered. David, on the other hand, loves shopping. When we were in New York, my mum said that she's never known a man like David. He will shop all day. And it's not all about himself. He'll look for things for other people, too. Like, if my sister's said she's been really looking for something, he'll spend all day trying to find it. He's really considerate and he'd never say, "Oh for god's sake, I want to get home!" In fact, he's the first to say, "Let's carry on." And he's got loads more clothes than I have.

Melanie C

We went into Versace in Italy, which was great, even though clothes don't interest me much. I like to be comfy and casual and every now and then I like to dress up, but I'm not usually that bothered about what I look like. I wear make-up to make myself look a bit better, but I'd rather not. It annoys me. Whenever I can avoid wearing it, I will.

Victoria

I've never actually worn this dress, even though I really like it. Still, I'll wear it at some point. This was in the Versace shop in Milan. We got on really well with Donatella and she did all the suits for the footballers for the European Cup final. I really like this picture because you can see David there. In fact, I've got it up in my house.

Melanie G

We went to the Versace shop and were allowed to pick three outfits each, which was very nice. I ended up trying to nick some sunglasses as well and got caught! They just said, "Here, have them." It was pretty embarrassing.

Melanie C

Da da! I'm showing off because I'm wearing an England training top that David gave me.

I enjoyed wearing all my different shirts everywhere we went. When we were in America I wore a different basketball or hockey shirt for every show. Europe was the best for shirts because I wore nothing but soccer shirts. It was funny when we played Manchester, because I wore my Liverpool shirt and half the audience cheered and the other half booed.

Melanie C

Having your hair and make-up done every day drives you mad. It was nice at first, a bit like being pampered, but the novelty wore off. The hair and make-up people make you look really, really special, but when you have to sit there for two hours - because it can take an hour for hair and an hour for make-up - especially when you're tired and someone's poking and touching at your face and your hair, you just want to scream, "Get off me!!!" But the end result's always good, so you just have to grin and bear it. It's like being on a long flight. You just have to think, right, it's for a good cause, so just chill out and relax.

Victoria

I can do my own make-up and I often make myself up. But generally speaking I look terrible most of the time. I'm not one of these people who can get out of bed and look great, like Natalie Imbruglia. I imagine that she looks great all the time, but I'm not like that. David looks the same all the time. He wakes up in the morning and looks like he's just done a front cover, whereas I need hair and make up – or a hat.

Having your hair and make-up done before every show did get a bit tedious. I'm afraid I'm not very professional about it and if I'm in downtown Texas where I don't know anybody, I'll go on stage in my pyjamas and not care (although I never did, of course!) But Melanie C always used to look her best. Some days I'd think, so what if I leave my trademark necklace on or off? Or, I don't even want to put any make up on to go on stage tonight. I don't know anyone in Texas, so it doesn't matter.

Emma

Playing basketball with the dancers was brilliant fun, but we had to tell the boys off at one point because they were getting injured playing it before shows.

Melanie G

Jim started the basketball off, but it had to stop because the dancers were getting injured left, right and centre. Then Emma decided to monitor it and join in herself.

Melanie C

It's quite a usual sight to see us in the back of a car, on the phone. The back of the car is my office. That's the only time I ever speak to anyone on the phone, because if I'm anywhere else, I'm doing something. And now I'm driving myself a lot more, I'm not getting to speak to as many people.

Victoria

David's physio told him the reason his neck was bad was because he spends so much time on the phone. Seriously, it's a problem with him. I'm not particularly sociable and I don't like to be out all the time, but I'm not very good at being totally on my own. So my phone bills were phenomenal. We got these phone calling cards when we were out there which literally cut a third off your bill, but I still spent a fortune.

Emma

The phone was our life in America. We had a right nightmare at the beginning of the tour there, when they gave us some phones that weren't working. They didn't work for a couple of weeks and we were like, "We need phones!" And we had huge phone bills by the end, especially Victoria.

Victoria

It was very hard to leave David behind. When you go away, you can't help but worry about where the other person is. Are they going out? What are they doing? We've got a lot of trust in each other, but it's always in the back of your mind when you're so far away.

David's never been a bloke's bloke. He goes out with his friends for a drink, but he's not one of those men who will go out and stay out all night without ringing. It's not an unwritten rule, it's just an unwritten way of life, really. Whenever I go out, even if it's 3 o'clock in the morning when I get in, I'll ring David just to let him know that I'm home safely. It's just so that he doesn't wake up in the morning and think, did she get home? Did her driver run off with her? Or whatever. So we always ring to let each other know we've got home. Every time he went out while I was on tour, he'd phone me and say, "I'm in the restaurant now and I'm just ordering my starter. Speak to you later." Then, ten minutes later, it's like, "Right I've had my starter now, what do you think I should have for my main course? Shall I have chicken, fish or steak?" It sounds silly, but it was literally like that.

Victoria (On tour 1998)

Everyone used to ask if my initial attraction to David was the fact that he was famous. I always said it wasn't, but actually that was a lie. If someone is really talented, as a footballer or an artist or an academic, the point isn't that they are famous, but that they are talented and dedicated. That is an attraction in itself. Of course, the fact that we are in the same position makes us equal and it is quite ironic the way our careers run parallel. When we first met, I was on my first album and he was playing in his first proper first team season. Then I went on tour and did another album and he played in the World Cup. When we had the trauma over Geri, he kicked someone in the World Cup and got slaughtered for that - every time something goes wrong for one of us, the other gets a problem too.

It's quite good really, because we can help each other out. I've seen all the bad press David's had. It's been awful. His mum and dad can comfort him and tell him not to worry, but really the only one who understands is me. That's because we've had a terrible time with the press, especially over the split with Simon Fuller. So I really am the only other person who can relate to him, because I have been through it too.

Melanie C (On tour 1998)

I think the reason I am not in a relationship is because I am far too focused on work and I would probably resent anything that took my focus away from it. But sometimes I do miss having someone.

I realised today for the first time that I am, or was, very, very shy. But Melanie pointed out to me the other day that I'm not so shy anymore. I think we have all grown up a lot and learnt a lot from each other. We've all taken on some of each other's traits, too. For instance, when we first got together, I was very shy and quiet and Mel B was very loud and aggressive. But now she has chilled out a little bit (although she is still very loud and dangerous) and I have become more talkative and cheeky.

Melanie C

I remember that feeling of sheer exhaustion, when you don't know how you're going to get through the next show and you don't know how you do, but you just do. I think you run on adrenaline until you go out on stage, when the fans feed you so much energy that you get through it. Then you get on the tour bus and go back to looking pretty vacant.

Victoria

Looking back, the tour was very tiring. I enjoyed Europe more than I did America, but I think that was partly because I found out I was pregnant in America and had a lot of morning sickness. So the American bit was more difficult for me, plus David couldn't be with me much, so it was very lonely at times. But Europe was great fun. It felt so good to be able to get up and sing finally, after spending so much time doing promotion and interviews. Up until then, performing was quite a small part of what we actually did, so to get up there and sing was the best feeling ever.

Looking at these pictures as we're coming off the coach, it reminds me of how every day after we'd finished the show, we'd quickly put on our dressing gowns, get on the coach, take off all our make-up and get off the coach looking sweaty and disgusting! Often we'd forget that there were going to be photographers at the other end, waiting to snap us looking hideous.

Emma

Often, we'd do a runner straight from the stage into our coach, so that we could leave the stadium before the roads got jammed up. We'd get changed on the coach, have a laugh, take all our make up off and talk about who went wrong that night. There were often paparazzi waiting for us when we went back to our hotel after a show. But sometimes we'd forget they'd be there and take all our make up off on the coach, either because we were going to bed or getting ready to go out.

Melanie C

When we were in Paris, we were coming off the tour bus to go into our hotel when we saw that there were loads of fans and press outside. We'd all taken all our make-up off and messed up our hair, so we looked terrible. Because we knew we were going to have our pictures taken, we did a Michael Jackson for a joke. Then we understood why he keeps his face covered – because he's not had time to do his make-up! So that was our Michael Jackson impression, which we thought was hilarious and no one else really did (like most of our jokes).

Melanie C

There were many happy times spent on that tour bus. That's when we used to have the most fun - travelling to and from the venues in it. We'd always get giggling fits and be really silly, because we were so tired. When you're that tired, you're delirious, so most of our time on the bus was spent just laughing at things that weren't really that funny.

Victoria

I remember this day in New York very well. I was pregnant, my mum and dad were about to come and see me and I did a photo shoot with Dean in the police station. I didn't know I was pregnant because this was the day before my mum came out, bringing the test with her.

Melanie C

I had a great time the day I went to Chinatown, even though it stank to high heaven. It was really, really hot and there were loads of fruit and vegetable stalls - I think it was the fresh fish stalls that stank so much - and it was very interesting to see such a different culture. A whole little China in the centre of New York.

We were in New York for a week so we had time to explore it properly, but we didn't even stay overnight in a lot of the other places, which was a shame. I'm very, very interested in America and always have been, since I was a kid. We're brought up on American movies and TV, so it was nice to go there and see it for real. It's such a huge place and, as they say, every state is like a different country. I love it there.

I didn't enjoy Europe as much because of the language barriers. I can't stand not being able to be understood. I've just cracked the American thing now - because sometimes you may as well be speaking a different language to American people, even though you're speaking English. The trick is to talk slowly and use Americanisms.

Emma

I think David and Victoria are a fabulous couple. When those two met, it made me believe in love again, it really did. I hadn't had a boyfriend for a while and obviously my parents weren't together and I hadn't seen two people so totally and utterly in love for a very long time. At the Versace party the other day Victoria was talking to me but still holding hands with David. They never want to let go of each other. I just love that.

Victoria

After one of the stadium concerts, I changed into my dressing gown and drove back to Manchester with David. I took my make up off in the car and then David needed to fill up with some petrol, so we pulled over. I got out and while I was standing there waiting to pay for some sweets, I turned round and all of a sudden there were hundreds of camera flashes. We'd been followed to the petrol station by a load of photographers and the next day it was all over the papers. Luckily they only got the back of me. But still, I was wearing a dressing gown that said Posh on the back and a pair of Nikes and my hair was all over the place because I'd been wearing a wig on stage. I looked horrendous! The headline said something like, How Posh is this? A bag of sweets and a dressing gown. But we loved our dressing gowns, especially because David asked Adidas to make them for us.

I like to go out, but I'm not the sort of person who goes to clubs every night. I mean, I enjoy going out with my friends but I don't do it that often. When we're on tour, I'm often quite tired after a show and then I just want to go and sleep, because I like to get up and do things during the day. You visit so many different countries and you get a flavour of each place even if you just have a wander round the streets for an hour. But if you go out at night, you end up lying in and missing out on that.

I'd say that Melanie G and Emma were probably the most sociable on tour, if you see it in terms of going to all the parties and meeting famous people. I didn't do that very much. Typically, after a show I'd go into my hotel room, sit down, put the telly on, order all my room service, put all my food around me, eat like a horse and then be on the phone for 5 hours. All the tax money I saved by taking a year out literally went on phone calls. I'd just be on the phone to David all the time, discussing what I was eating and what I was watching on the telly for hours and hours and hours.

Melanie C

Victoria really, really missed David and they love each other so much that it was a relief when he came out to visit. It made her so happy to see him. When he wasn't there, we kept her company and had fun, but it wasn't the same. She particularly wanted him near when she was pregnant. She wanted Daddy to be there. We all get on really well with him. He's a lovely bloke. We've welcomed him into the Spice family with open arms, as we did Jim.

Melanie C

Mel fancied Jim from the minute she saw him. She said, "He's mine!" and she was right. He was very professional, as were all the dancers. They knew not to go there. They didn't want relationships with any of the Girls and we didn't want relationships with any of them. But Jim took Melanie's eye and when she decides she wants something, she goes out and she gets it. So Jim made sure all the dancers were cool about things, and she made sure that all us girls had accepted him and eventually they got together. We just wanted them both to be happy, so it was really nice.

At first we were very protective, because you hear a lot of stories about dancers who do the rounds - you get a lot of charmers. But Jim obviously loves Mel and that's what counts. Melanie is so professional - we all are - and we knew that if it ever became a problem, we would have dealt with it. But it didn't. It's not worth worrying about something until it's worth worrying about, is it?

Melanie G

I knew I was going to marry Jim the first day I met him. We'd just flown back from some promotion somewhere and we were all knackered, when the other Girls said: "Let's go and meet the dancers!" I tried to put it off to the next day, because I wanted to look good when I met them, but the others said: "NO, we have to see them NOW. We've got rehearsals with them tomorrow and it's important to meet up before we start working with them." So we went. I remember looking at Jim and thinking, Oh, WOW, then putting my jacket up to hide my face because I had no make-up on. I knew he was the one straight away, but it took me about three months to get him.

I was on a mission, but he wasn't having any of it. The first routine we rehearsed was 'Do it', where you're literally all over each other. I felt such an attraction that I couldn't even look at Jim, but he wasn't at all shy with me. He said: "Come on then, show me what you're made of!" I just giggled meekly. I was crap when I started dancing and I still feel a bit self-conscious when I dance in front of him, even now.

It's funny because we'd only been seeing each other for a little while when the tour manager told me that one of the Sheffield concerts was scheduled for 13th September. I'd already decided to get married that day, if Jim and I were still together, even though it was ages away. I don't know how I knew, I just did. So I asked the tour manager to change the dates of the gigs, without explaining why.

It didn't happen instantly between Jim and me because I was with somebody and he was with somebody and we didn't want to get together in a dishonest way. For a while we were just really good friends and hung out with each other a lot. When that changed, we decided we wanted to keep business and pleasure apart, because mixing them can always make things go a little bit sour. But after a while, I said to the Girls: "Look I can't help it. You can tell me to stop it and I'll try to, but at the end of the day, I can't stop what I feel". And they said: "Okay, but make sure it doesn't interfere with your work."

It only interfered once, after we'd had a bit of an argument. It was time for Do It and I came on stage and said: "You're a shit!" in front of everyone. That was just me being, you know, whatever. One of the reasons Jim didn't want to get together with me was that, because we manage ourselves, I - or the Girls - could sack him at any moment. He proposed in Paris, at the Buddha Bar, where we'd had our first date. I went to meet him there, but when I sat down, there was a big bunch of flowers in his seat. I waited and waited and eventually I read the card that came with the flowers - the lyrics of the Luther Vandross song 'You're The Only One'. Soon Jim walked in. He'd already ordered for me - exactly what I'd eaten when we first went there. Then he got down on one knee. I said: "What are you doing?" He said: "Will you..." and I said: "Yes!" and he gave me this ring, which says 'to be or not to be' on it.

Later, I went back to my room and the whole suite was filled with lilies. They were everywhere - hanging from the ceiling, on the lights and all over the bed. It was amazing. I rushed into Emma's room, woke her up and said: "I've just got engaged!" She was, like, "Whaaat!?"

Working together made it all the more exciting, really. We'd see each other a little bit before the show, but with so many people around we couldn't just sneak off, even though we did a few times. It was great the way we'd see each other and then we'd separate, then we'd see each other on stage again and have to be very professional - although one time I really lost the plot and started to kiss him on stage.

Melanie G

As 2 Become 1 moved into the reggae section, Jim and I used to have a little bit of a vibe together and it ended up where I would just grab his neck. But then he started to grab me back. We'd do this thing where we'd grab each other in all the spots that drive you crazy. We were always in hysterics.

Victoria

I was really happy when Mel and Jim got together. I suppose it was a bit strange at first, because he was a dancer on the tour, but I'm an old romantic, so I just didn't have a problem with it. A lot of people said that they were rushing into it but I know I'd have got engaged to David the first week I met him. Sometimes you just know when you've met the right person. Well, that's the way it happened for me, anyway. I just want people to be happy, and if getting engaged made Melanie happy, then it was fine with me.

Victoria

When I was pregnant, I was convinced there was going to be something wrong. I'd had all the tests and everything seemed fine, but it's something you have very little control over. I mean, I didn't smoke or drink or do anything like that and they told me there was nothing to worry about. But I'm a real worrier. I worry about everything. So I'd think, what if there's something wrong? How can something you have no control over turn out to be so perfect? And even now when I look at him I'm just amazed at his feet, arms, legs, fingers, toes - every bit of him. He's a person! It's incredible to think that David and I made him. I was really, really careful on tour. We calmed down some of the dance routines

and tried to do whatever we could to make it easier on us, but it was hard. The hardest thing for me was the morning sickness. I had it all day, every day. I couldn't bear the smell of food. We used to get on this plane to travel from place to place and I couldn't bear the smell of the plane.

Everyone knows that you don't tell anyone you're pregnant until after the first three months, but somebody leaked it to the press somewhere along the line and it went in the papers. They took a picture of me by the swimming pool and I looked bigger in those photos than I did when they got pictures of me in my swimming costume five months on. I don't know if they enlarged my

stomach, or just took the photograph from a bad angle, but it was so, so difficult because I wasn't past three months and I hadn't told anybody. I looked at the papers and I thought, my goodness, what if something goes wrong? I felt it was really unfair because I wanted to wait until I'd come home and had all the scans. It's not every day that you have news like, "We're having a baby", but the privilege of telling our family and friends was taken away from us because somebody told the newspapers and the newspapers told everybody.

Then, of course, everybody wants to get a picture of you to see if you're pregnant. I remember seeing photos where they gave

Emma

I was aware of the attraction between Mel and Jim from the start because I was always on the bus with them. When he asked her to marry him in Paris they came straight into our room and told us. I think I was one of the first to know, which was lovely. It was quite mad, though. Like, "Oh! Melanie's getting engaged!" It was a bit of a surprise because they hadn't been together that long.

I'm very sensible and I always say things like, "Are you sure about this?" I always put a bleedin' dampener on everything! She was like, "Shut up you, I'm just doing it, okay?" And I said, "Just be aware, blah, blah, blah..." I'm like that with Mel about a lot of things.

She always says to me, "Well, other people would tell me to just do it!" and I say, "Well I'm not saying it because I want to put a dampener on it. I'm just worried about you personally and that's it."

But then my mum is such a worrier and sometimes I think, I hope I'm not too much like her in that way, because she does worry a lot and it can get her in a state at times. She won't go to sleep until I get in, which is very sweet and lovely, but it also puts some strain on her. I just think, Mum! You don't have to worry so much.

Emma

I was ecstatic when I heard that Mel and Victoria were pregnant. They were both in love and we were near the end of the tour, so it was perfect. Although it was still quite early on, we told them to take it as easy as they could. Obviously, we were prepared to do more to hype the show up and keep it balanced if they were feeling tired. They were so good because they were determined to finish the tour. I mean, if that was me I'd have gone, "Bye, I'm going home! I'm pregnant". But they were brilliant and determined and we finished every single show. We didn't cancel a single one through all of it, through Geri leaving and the girls getting pregnant.

Melanie G

My pregnancy was quite hard and very, very emotional. I think I felt a fear of the unknown, of what was going on in my head or my hormones. I wasn't working and we were living a bit on top of each other in a little cottage in the country. It was all a bit too much, but then I always think we have to go through bad bits to appreciate the good bits. Not everything in life is good and smooth.

Even though you don't realise it at the time, when you look back, you think, oh dear, I really was hormonal. Now I can look back and laugh, but when it was happening, I'd be shouting, "It's NOT because I'm pregnant, I MEAN it!"

me a lump I didn't actually have. I was in size eight jeans until I was five and a half months pregnant and I didn't look any different, yet I had a bump at two and a half months in the photos. You know, Posh Bump In America. It was crap because I didn't even have a bulge. I think Brooklyn was like a parasite living inside me - he ate everything!

I eat a lot more now I've had him. I used to eat mainly vegetables and fruit, whereas now I eat anything and everything and I couldn't go back to the way I was before. I don't know why I'm smaller now than before I got pregnant, but I think it must be because I'm running around all the time.

Victoria

I was always amazed at how Melanie used to go down the gym in the mornings. Sometimes I'd think, she's got to be mad! I couldn't do it myself. I'd love to. I'd love a six pack, but I just can't be bothered, so I'd rather cover up my tummy and eat more.

Victoria (On tour 1998)

Professionally, I'm really looking forward to recording the third album and working in England again. I love it when we go down to Elstree to do Top Of the Pops, and then onto Des O'Connor and Live and Kicking. I love it all, even the way home, driving down the Bayswater Road to my mum's house in London and it being all sunny. I might go and sit in the park or go and do some shopping, then go for dinner. On Saturday nights, just sitting in and watching Blind Date is like heaven for me.

Melanie G

When Victoria and I were first pregnant, every so often we'd have to ask someone to let our costumes out. Nobody knew why and we'd have to say: "We're just getting fat." For ages, the dressers thought I was just putting on weight. Then it got ridiculous because I'd have to have a plastic cup in my room to wee in. I needed to wee three or four times during the show and the toilets were miles away.

Melanie C (On tour 1998)

There's nothing in this world for me except music. I just want to be a singer and that's all I want to do for the rest of my life. The tour has just confirmed to me that if I did anything else I would be denying myself. And I know this sounds a bit sad, because it means there aren't many other things going on in my life, but I'm only truly happy when I'm on stage.

Getting up on stage makes the rest of your life seem a bit boring.... as the doors open and you see the crowd and all the cameras start flashing, you just can't help smiling. It's like being at the top of a roller coaster ride - then it goes whoosh and there's no turning back.

If you're a performer, you perform no matter what - whether it's for one person or one million. Of course, it doesn't exactly feel the same when I'm up in front of 20,000 people as it did when I was eight years old and tap dancing, but I'm still giving what I was giving then - I'm doing the same thing I've done all my life.

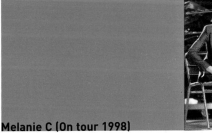

Melanie C (On tour 1998)

Over the last few years we have had a few traumatic things happen to the Spice Girls and to us personally and I think everything happens for a reason. During the tour I've learnt that although everybody is different, they all have the same needs and the same insecurities. Nobody wants to hurt anyone or upset them but, you know, sometimes things just happen. There are always two sides to every argument and who is to say who is wrong? If you believe in your argument, then you are right in your eyes.

The end of the tour - and Geri's departure - really seem to mark the end of an era. It's the beginning of the new Spice Girls and when we get home I feel I want to start a brand new life.

I like to think that the Spice Girls will go on forever. I think we will do lots of things individually which are exciting musically and also some TV and film work, but the five of us will always be great mates.

Melanie G

Phoenix has brought a lot of happiness. I wanted her to come so badly, just to have her there, so I think that's why she came early, I could feel her inside me and the kicks were getting stronger and stronger.

You feel quite alone when you're pregnant, because your man can't feel what it feels like. He can only feel all that life force developing inside you from the outside and the scans don't mean as much to him. It was much better when she arrived and he could get more involved. Now he's mad about Phoenix and loves being a dad.

AT HOME

Melanie C

We'd been away for so long and there were so many people to see when we got home that we were really quite busy when we got back to England. Then, as it all sunk in, it began to feel quite weird to be away from the others. But we'd been in each other's pockets for a long time and when someone's there all the time, you start to take them for granted. When they're not there, you realise how great they are and what a great time we had and how much you miss them, so then it's nice when we get back together - we really appreciate each other.

Emma

Although I like London, I prefer living outside the city. I stayed at Louie's the other night and we decided to walk into Covent Garden from Waterloo. It's the most exercise I've had for years! It's lovely to walk along the river bank and look at all the old buildings, but then I do like going home and having a good wash, because it's filthy in London.

Victoria

When I'm at home, David and I go out sometimes, but not a lot. That's because I like to spend most of the time with Brooklyn. Still, I think it's really important (and my mum's always telling me this, too) for the two of us to go out on our own every now and then. I hate leaving Brooklyn, but it's vital in a relationship to make sure that you spend time together as well. So sometimes it's really good to make yourselves get out and leave Brooklyn with his grandmother.

Melanie C

I went to loads of gigs in LA. I went to see Lenny Kravitz, who might be doing some work on my album. Whenever the Brits were in town, we went to see them. I saw Blur and Robbie Williams - both excellent gigs.

Emma

My friends have been really cool about me being away for so long and it's been really lovely to see them again. It's great because I'm still really good friends with Dawn, who I've known since I was four, and Donna and Alison, who I went to school with. I've really enjoyed catching up with people, talking about what they've been up to and telling them what I've done. It's funny when I meet old school friends who didn't have contact with me while I was doing Spice, but knew me before. They say things like, "You've come from being little Emma at school, being funny and doing silly school shows. Now you're back from a world tour!" It's really mad telling them all about it.

Melanie G

As soon as I came off tour, I got married. I moved into my house and went on honeymoon - it was like one big roller coaster ride again. Then I had a No.1 with Missy Elliot. It was a real mad time, with so many things happening at once, publicly. I started to miss those quiet Sundays where you can just chill and take in what's happened during the week.

Victoria

When we're out, I'm scared to put Brooklyn in a buggy or a pushchair because so often you'll get some photographer leap out and shove a camera in your face. I don't want to put him in that position, because I feel it's unfair. So I have to carry him and he's getting really heavy.

About a week and a half after Brooklyn was born, I was at the Bluewater shopping centre and all of a sudden I looked over and saw a bunch of photographers taking pictures of him as I was lifting him out of his pushchair. Suddenly I got 'paranoid mother syndrome', gave Brooklyn to my mother and chased them through the mall screaming and shouting. I nearly caught up with them, which is amazing, really, as I could hardly walk because of the Caesarian section. Everybody was looking round as if I'd shoplifted or something. Then I thought, oh dear, I'm lost, my back hurts, my tummy hurts, and I nearly collapsed on the floor. It was in the paper the next day, but they didn't get a clear picture of Brooklyn.

Emma

I love living with my mum, but I'm thinking of getting a house, maybe a weekend place where I can go and have all my mates round. I'm so lucky, because my mum does my washing and there's always someone around when you wake up, which is lovely. The dog's running about and you look out in the garden and your brother's mending something and it's great, I love it. But then again I do think that maybe at weekends when I go out with my friends, it would be nice to be able to invite them back to mine and have enough room for them all to stay. I don't know if I want to move out totally, but I'd just like to have a little retreat.

I do love it at home, though. For instance, I just loved it the other morning. It was boiling hot, I opened my door and my dog was sitting outside, waiting for me. My mum was swimming in the pool and my brother was doing a barbecue with his girlfriend. It was fab.

It was a bit like at Ronan's house in Ireland. He and his wife Yvonne, who I know quite well, invited me over. He was doing a gig, so I went to the gig and we went out to dinner and I stayed at theirs. Yvonne is lovely and when I woke up in the morning, she was there with the baby and Ronan's two brothers were there, too, plus Yvonne's brother and the mum. I love all that. I love waking up with people around.

My mum and I are a lot like flatmates. She'll tell me she's having friends over and I'm like, "Okay! I'm out." Or I'll tell her that I'm having some friends over and she'll say, "Okay, I'll go and stay at my boyfriend's." It's really good. My brother's girlfriend lives with us now and that's lovely because we have a laugh. Sometimes when my brother goes out, she stays in and we watch Friends together and chat.

Emma

Since I've been back, I've been to quite a few parties, like the Versace party. It's just lots of people dressed in Versace, with lots of press trying to find out the gossip and people you don't know asking you for pictures. You don't really have real conversations unless you take your mates along. I was at the Versace party for half an hour and then I decided to go. Obviously, that kind of event is very glamorous, but it's not my sort of thing. It's easier for David and Victoria because they're together, so they can sort of protect each other.

I prefer going out with friends and just having a laugh with people I know. We'll go for something to eat and then maybe go for a drink - that sort of thing. I've been catching up on all that since I got back, because I haven't done it for so long. I mean, I went straight from school to college and joined the Girls when I was 18, so I missed that partying stage.

Victoria

Brooklyn wasn't really planned, but looking back on it now, it was the perfect time in our relationship. It was also a good time for me to have a baby because we were all coming home in September and having a bit of a break anyway. If I hadn't had him when I did, I would have had to wait until after the tour next year. And then, of course, it takes another year to make a baby. So, for me it was perfect timing. The other Girls went off to do their own individual things, whereas I wanted to spend time at home with my family and Brooklyn. To me that's a priority, you know. When I was pregnant, I went through quite a lot of stress, what with being away, working and all the media attention. So it was just nice to be at home, finally.

Also, I wanted to be a young mum - especially because I want to have more than one child - and I just felt it was the right time for me in my life and David in his. It was something that we really thought long and hard about, though. Even now, I can hardly believe that I had Brooklyn. I have to keep pinching myself when I look at him.

Melanie G

For four years, since I'd moved to London, I'd mostly been living out of a suitcase, but when I came back from tour, I finally had somewhere to call my own and life became a lot more stable. I don't really see my house as a huge mansion - it's just my base, my retreat. But even now, when I walk down to the end of the garden and look back, it still takes my breath away.

Melanie G

I think you can have the best of both worlds - you can definitely go out and work and do your thing as well as being a good mum. Phoenix will be coming into the studio with me - not for the whole day, but for an hour or so every day. I miss her too much otherwise. I've only been away from her once, for ten days in America, and it killed me. I can never leave her to cry, either, but once she's asleep, I know I can relax. I'm not like one of those paranoid mothers who can't get on with her life - if she wakes up, I'll just stick her on my hip, walk round with her and do what I have to do.

Victoria

I remember when Brooklyn was first born, it was such a shock to the system. The first five weeks he had terrible colic and was awake every minute of the day. As soon as he opened his eyes, he'd be screaming. He never just sat there. The washing you get through if you've got a sicky baby is incredible - you use up ten outfits a day and you're washing all the time. You never get to sit down because as soon as the baby's asleep, you've got a thousand things to do. I planned on going down the gym to get back into shape, but I've got no hope of that because I don't have five minutes to go to the toilet. Even when I'm having a wee, I think, come on, hurry up!

Still, you have to make sure the baby fits into your life, rather than you adapting your life to a baby. We've got friends who have children and their life purely revolves around the kids. But I hope Brooklyn's going to learn to be a bit more flexible. He's going to come on tour with me and there are going to be times when he's at my mum's and other times when he's in Manchester.

Victoria

I was quite a natural mother from the start. Whereas my sister breastfed for a week and then put Liberty on the bottle, I was a bit of an earth mother. I did everything by the book and expressed the milk and all the rest of it. I actually really liked breastfeeding, but Brooklyn was just getting so hungry that I couldn't keep up with him. He needed feeding all the time and I was exhausted.

Melanie C

Working out gives me more energy and I make sure I eat well and take loads of vitamins. I always carry loads of fruit in my bag, in case I need a boost. It was cool on tour because we had catering, so we could always have whatever we wanted. The caterers were great and really looked after us - they brought loads of our favourite food over from England for us.

I'm body building at the moment, so I'm eating about six meals a day. Obviously you can't sit down to a table and eat six meals a day so I'll have a protein shake for breakfast and a mid-morning snack, like some fruit. I have a proper lunch and then, when those mid-afternoon hunger pangs appear at around 4pm, I have another shake. I have a proper meal in the evening and I may eat again at about 10 or 11 o'clock.

I eat lots of fish and lots of vegetables and I've started eating chicken again. I did want to be vegetarian but it's too hard, because I'm trying to become more muscular and vegetable protein like soya is great, but it's just not got the same density as fish. Fish is the best because it contains oils which are really good for your joints and skin. When I was a vegetarian, I wasn't getting enough protein. I'd have loads of beans and pulses, which are great because they contain protein and carbs, but they just weren't enough, especially for lifting weights and body building.

I've started bodybuilding because I want to be strong. Of course, I love the muscle definition, but my main aim is to be stronger. You know when you've got a heavy bag and a bloke says, "Let me help you with that"? Well, I like to be able to carry my own bags. I like to be able to open jam jars without having to ask a boy to do it for me. While I was in LA I worked out a lot and learnt how to swim doing all the proper strokes. I also brushed up on my kick boxing techniques and did loads of yoga.

I'm the sort of person who goes from one extreme to the other. There are times when I've not looked after myself. I was very unhappy when I was unemployed and I didn't take the same kind of care of myself then. I was going in no direction, but then as soon as I found my direction, I was fine. But every now and then, I go the other way again. I party too much and get run down. That's what happened after we came off tour. I think it was because life seems so boring after you've been on the road.

Melanie G

When we're not working, Jim and I do things like take the dogs for a walk, have a stroll around Marlowe, go shopping and out for dinner. We don't have a problem with the other one going out with their mates, either. Our relationship is quite open and free, really.

I want Brooklyn to have as much of an ordinary life as he can, but obviously, I'm going to be sensible about it as well. When we go on holiday, it's not easy for us to go to a hotel and just sit on the beach. I mean, we could do, but I don't really like Brooklyn being photographed.

He's going to be really well behaved, because I hate naughty children. I absolutely can't stand them. He's not going to be a spoilt brat. Obviously it's going to be difficult because David buys him everything, but when he

Victoria

Even now, I speak to David probably around ten times a day if we're not together - and at least one of those conversations is always over an hour long. I don't know what we find to talk about. We just talk, talk, talk, talk, talk, all the time. We've always had a lot in common.

People always say how important it is for partners to have a good friendship - and we have. I talk about the same sorts of things to David as I do to my best friend, because he's like a good friend as well. A lot of people seem to think he's a bit dim and doesn't say much, but when you get to know him and his feelings, he's actually quite deep. Nobody else apart from me sees that, which is quite nice, in a way.

David's very shy and rarely speaks about his feelings to anyone apart from me. We agree on most things, but he's very opinionated as well, even though a lot of people don't realise it. He's definitely not a walkover. He knows what he wants and he wouldn't let anybody get away with anything.

Even though I'm quite independent, I'm quite old-fashioned. I wouldn't just say: "I'm going out with my friends tonight, so stick that up your bum." He never minds me going out, but I say: "Look, do you mind? Can you look after baby?" I'm not one of these women who feels the need just to do her own thing, without respecting anybody else.

gets bigger he's going to have to learn that he's not just going to pass his test and get a BMW convertible. I want him to learn the value of money, understand that he's a very lucky boy and that it's not everybody who has what he has. I want him to be totally in touch with reality.

Melanie G

I'm going back to America in October to do some more work on my album. It's really good self-expression - I've written songs about my childhood and what's going on in my life now. My voice has definitely changed - it's got a different tone to it now and I can sing high notes. I'm not going to be able to cop out of the high harmonies anymore. In fact, Emma pulled me up on that the other day, so I've got no more excuses.

Melanie C

I'm very, very selfish right now, which is probably why I haven't met anyone. It's all about me at the moment, so I couldn't have a child either, because I just don't think I could be responsible enough. If I do meet someone it's because it's meant to happen, but I'm not out looking for it.

It's great because I've got nobody else to answer to. I think a lot of that stems from the fact that my mum and dad got divorced when I was 3 and they both went on to have children in other marriages. I've always been a part of both families, but growing up as a child I felt as though I didn't really belong to either. That's probably what's made me so independent.

Melanie G

It was really weird to be away from the other Girls at first. It was 70% weird and 30% really nice. I just dived into moving into my house and decorating, but it was strange waking up and thinking, what have I got to do today? I've got to phone Emma's room, check Melanie and speak to Victoria. Then I'd realise that I didn't have to do any of that because I was at home in my own bed. That took a bit of getting used to.

Melanie C

When the tour finished, it was in the back of my mind that I wanted to do some solo work and it's worked out better than I could have dreamed. I've had a brilliant time recording it in LA and I am really pleased with it.

I've been lucky enough to have had a musical background. I used to listen to my mum's albums - loads of the Beatles and Stevie Wonder and all the Tamla Motown stuff. There was even Deep Purple and Led Zeppelin in her collection, so I've always listened to a bit of a mad cross-section of music, including classical music. I never studied much as a kid because I was too interested in my dancing, but I think I must have soaked up a load of stuff anyway. I've never read to widen my vocabulary or anything like that, so I really surprised myself when I was working on my lyrics.

Melanie C

It's been madness trying to get the album together in time. I'm in the final stages of mixing it now. There's so much happening every day that it's really hard to stay on top of it all. There are people doing string arrangements in one studio, I'm finishing off vocals in another studio, somebody's mixing another song in another part of town and then I'm darting in and out listening to mixes. It's pretty hectic, but LA is a great town to make a record in. There are so many studios and musicians. I've already worked in six or seven studios - there seem to be two massive, full-blown studios on every block in Hollywood!

Victoria

When David knows I'm at a game, he always likes to see me before he starts playing. At the Barcelona game he was walking round the pitch, looking everywhere for me. All of David's friends who knew I was going to be there were also looking round saying, "Where the hell is she?" David was worried because he thought I'd been stranded at the airport or got lost. It was worse than that because my ticket hadn't been left at my hotel and only after loads of hassle would they let me in the ground. Just as they were about to start, I walked down the stairs with my hair all over the shop, wearing great big sunglasses because I had mascara all over my face. Still, as soon as he saw me, he relaxed. So I got there just in time.

Melanie G

Our wedding was absolutely amazing. We hadn't moved into the house yet, but we still had it in the grounds. It was a nice way to start off family life.

Victoria

At first, I didn't necessarily want a massive wedding and to be honest, I'd have got married sat here today, but it's going to be the only big wedding in our family. At the end of the day, it's lucky we did sell our pictures to OK! because we couldn't have handled the security aspect ourselves anyway. The media have created such a build-up to it that it's good we've had the support of the magazine to sort things out. Basically, I've told the co-ordinator what I want and we've really gone to town and had a laugh with it.

I'll be sitting on a great big throne with red and purple carpet everywhere. You know, if I didn't do something like that, they'd slate me for not doing it. So in the end I thought, I'm doing what I think everybody will enjoy and it's not all just exactly what I'd like. If I'd had everything I wanted, I'd have had R&B and soul and dance music in the evening, but I've got music for everybody and food for everybody. I can't stand little picky bits of food, so it's a proper dinner, like a Christmas dinner.

My dress is going to the Victoria & Albert Museum. They asked for it and I decided that it would be great if they made it into a charity thing. So if they want it, they have to give a donation to the Meningitis Trust, so it doesn't look quite so, "Here's my dress!" and it will have a purpose behind it as well. There are so many cynical people out there, particularly journalists, and I'd never want anyone to think, "Who do they think they are?".

A lot of people expected me to have some tight slinky little number for my wedding dress, but it's totally the opposite. It's very Scarlett O'Hara, because that's what I always wanted.

Victoria

It's weird because we just think of ourselves as pretty normal and we plod about at home and dress really casually. Then we go out and photographers go berserk. The next day, we're like, "What do we look like in the paper?" Of course, you can't live like that and you just take it with a pinch of salt, but I suppose that's part of what it's all about. What are they going to say about us? Still, you know that if they say you're fat and ugly, you wouldn't exactly sit and cry about it, because it's just somebody's opinion.

Victoria

The other day a friend came round for a drink, with another friend and her two year old daughter. When they got home, the little girl apparently said "I spent the day with baby Broccoli" The name has kind of stuck now - my little lump of broccoli! I definitely, definitely want more children, but not just yet. Then again, I believe in fate. Sometimes things aren't planned and if it happens, it happens.

Melanie G

Phoenix is a real character. She looks exactly like Jim and she's got real attitude when she looks at you. But then again, she's a giggler and a nutter, too. She has really quiet moments and real mad moments when she just screams and talks and kicks.

Victoria

I'll do my own thing at some other point, definitely. Obviously I've got ambitions, but I'm happy with what I've got at the moment!

Melanie C

As a child, I used to try my best at everything because I felt like a bit of a spare part and wanted to be extra special to make my mum and dad love me and to deserve their love and attention. Even now, I have a strong sense of not ever wanting to let anybody down.

Emma

I've never been a workaholic, I've never been a mad partier. I just do things in moderation. I've had a couple of weeks when I've gone out and seen friends and had a really good time and now I think, okay, I'm gonna stay at home with my family for a while. But then I worry that I'm being lazy.

Melanie C

I like to work hard. There's so much that needs to be done and life's short. Doing my album has been totally different, because it's been my own thing. The success of the Spice Girls, which the five of us created together, has enabled me to work with some amazing people. Everybody wants to work with the Spice Girls. I'm dead lucky like that, so I've really made the most of it

Victoria

I might not do any individual projects until next year. I don't want to rush into things, I want to make sure I'm doing the right thing. I'd like to do some acting and if I took on a bad role, it could do me more harm than good.

Emma

Recently I've been working with some producers called Tin Tin Out. They're really good fun. They've done stuff with the Corrs and they're just about to work with Salt'n'Pepper, but they're also artists in their own right. I did one track with them and they said they'd like to write with me, which I'd love.

I really want to do a solo album, but I want to take my time with it. I'm the kind of person who, if I'm ready to do something, then I just do it. So obviously I'm not quite ready, or I'd already be doing it! I was thinking about it the other day. The thing is, I like to write about my experiences and what I've been through. We've already written about the touring side of things and now I feel it's time to live at home, learn about myself, spend time with my friends and have different people around me so that I can to go in and write some good tracks. I want to write about how I've been coping and what I've learnt about myself, being back home, things like that.

Melanie G

It looks as though next year everything will be exploding. The Spice album will be released, my solo album will also be coming out and I really want to go on tour again. The other day I was talking to Emma about how we left out a big part of the world on the last tour. I definitely think we should go to South America, Japan and Australia next time. If we did, I guess we'd be performing old material as well as new. It would be a good mixture, anyway. Wherever we go, I'm really looking forward to getting up on stage again.

Melanie C

It's nearly six months since we worked together, so I'm really looking forward to getting back into the studio with the others.

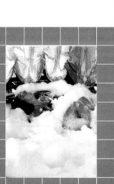

Melanie G

I'm really looking forward to the dates in December. It's mad to think that they sold out so quickly. It's also going to be fun to record together after such a long time. Although it might be quite strange at first to meet up in that kind of environment again. Emma will have been in the recording studio by herself and so will Melanie and I. When you're by yourself, you can call the shots, but when you're together you have to compromise and feed off each other to get the right kind of juices flowing.

Melanie C

I think everything happens at a certain time for a certain reason and that's just the way it is. Life's just like one long play. I've been to psychics in the past, but I don't bother anymore. I just look forward to the future. It's very exciting.

Abbey Road Studios, London. August 1999.

A LITTLE, BROWN BOOK

First published in Great Britain in 1999
by Little, Brown and Company (UK)

The Spice Girls would like to thank
David Beckham
Jimmy Gulzar
Jade Jones
Louie Spence
Carmine Canuso
Eszteca Noya
Robert Nurse
Christian Horsfall
Takao Baba
Alan Cumming
Vernon Hamilton
John Poole
Andy Bishop
NYPD
Richard Jones
Kenny Ho
Karin Darnell
Jennie Roberts
Simon Ellis
Andy Gangadeen
Paul Gendler
Fergus Gerrand
Steve Lewinson
Michael Martin
Andrew Thompson
Mike Brookes
Virgin Records
Nancy Phillips
Julie Cooke
Jamie Vickery
Julia Curnock
Jo Allen
Ying

Photography by Dean Freeman
Words by The Spice Girls and Rebecca Cripps
Design by Alexander Boxill
and Jean-Michel Dentand @ Grace

Edited and produced by Grace

A CIP catalogue for this book is available from the British Library

ISBN 0-316-85361-5

Printed and bound in the UK by Butler and Tanner Limited

Little, Brown and Company (UK)
Brettenham House
Lancaster Place
London WC2E 7EN